Cybersecurity for Normal People (Like You and Me)

A Practical Guide to Staying Safe Online

Charles Montago

Table of Contents

Introduction

Imagine you wake up one morning, grab your coffee, and sit down to check your email. Suddenly, you notice a series of suspicious messages. Your heart skips a beat. "Oh crap!" you think, realizing you've been hacked. This moment isn't just a nightmare for tech geeks or large corporations—it's happening to ordinary people like you and me every single day.

From innocent individuals discovering their bank accounts have been drained to those having their pictures or information leaked online without their consent, these are not isolated incidents but everyday occurrences in our increasingly digital world. Cybersecurity breaches have become more frequent than you might realize.

Consider your digital life an extension of your physical world. You wouldn't leave your front door open, inviting anyone to walk in and take whatever they please. Yet, many of us do just that with our online presence. Cybersecurity is not just a technical issue but a form of self-defense essential for protecting our identities, finances, and personal information.

Protecting your online presence is as crucial as locking your doors and setting up home security systems. It's about creating strong passwords, being cautious of phishing attempts, and understanding privacy settings on social media. In today's world, where we have a significant online footprint, cybersecurity is as vital as locking your doors at night.

You're in the right place if you've been looking to improve your cybersecurity knowledge. "Cybersecurity for Normal People (Like You and Me): A Practical Guide to Staying Safe Online" promises a straightforward, plain English approach. You don't need to be a tech whiz to understand the concepts and apply the tips provided here. We're focusing on practical, actionable steps that you can take immediately to enhance your security.

Our goal is to equip you with the knowledge and tools you need to stay safe in the digital world. This guide covers cybersecurity essentials, from recognizing phishing scams to understanding two-factor authentication. Each chapter will break down complex topics into easy-to-follow advice you can quickly adopt.

We'll start by demystifying cybersecurity, explaining why it matters, and showing that it's easier than you think. You'll meet the usual suspects, such as viruses, malware, and phishing, and learn how to become your own "human firewall" by adopting a security mindset.

We'll move on to learn how to build solid digital defenses. We'll investigate creating strong passwords, identifying sketchy websites, and securing your devices. You'll also learn about backups, encryption, and privacy settings to safeguard your precious information.

Moving further, we'll equip you with tips for the safe use of public Wi-Fi, protecting your devices while traveling, and steps to take if your device is lost or stolen.

But what if things go wrong? We've included a comprehensive guide for recognizing signs of trouble, taking immediate damage control steps, and reporting cybercrimes. You'll also find simple steps to create your own cybersecurity plan.

So, whether you're a parent looking to protect your family's online activities, a small business owner wanting to secure your transactions, or simply someone who wants peace of mind, this guide is for you. Let's embark on this journey together and transform that "Oh crap!" moment into a confident "I've got this!" Ready to hop in? Let's get started on making your online world a safer place!

Chapter 1:

Cybersecurity Crash Course

Let's start our journey by stripping away the tech jargon and revealing why cybersecurity is essential for everyone, not just IT professionals. If you've thought cybersecurity is all about complicated codes and high-tech solutions, then you are wrong. It's about ensuring your digital life is as safe as your physical one. We'll explore cybersecurity, why it matters, and how it impacts your daily activities, from online shopping to social media.

We'll also look at the usual suspects in cyber threats and discuss how you can become your first line of defense. By the end of this chapter, you'll have a solid foundation in cybersecurity basics, empowering you to take control of your online safety confidently.

What is Cybersecurity?

Cybersecurity simply means protecting interconnected networks and servers from cyber threats. It encompasses the steps taken by individuals and companies to prevent illegal access to their data centers and computerized systems.

It's like having a digital security system for your online world. Just as you lock your home to keep out intruders, cybersecurity helps protect your computers, smartphones, and personal information from hackers, viruses, and other online threats. It's about being cautious of dangers, using strong passwords, avoiding suspicious emails, and updating your software regularly. In short, it's all your steps to ensure your digital life is safe and secure. Protect your digital life with deliberate steps to ensure its safety and security.

Why Does Cybersecurity Matter?

Cybersecurity matters now more than ever because digital technologies are making our world increasingly interconnected. Ensuring your data and systems are protected from cyber threats becomes essential as we rely on these technologies for everything from communication to commerce. Here are some reasons why cybersecurity is vital:

Protection of Personal Information

Our data—such as financial details, health records, and private communications—is precious. Cybersecurity measures help prevent this sensitive information from being accessed by third parties, protecting us from identity theft and fraud.

Financial Security

Cyberattacks can lead to significant financial losses, not just through direct theft but also from the costs associated with recovery and potential business disruption. For individuals, cybersecurity helps protect bank accounts and financial assets from cybercriminals.

Operational Integrity

For businesses, cybersecurity ensures that operations run smoothly. A minor breach can disrupt services, leading to a loss of productivity. Effective cybersecurity helps maintain business continuity, protect intellectual property, and prevent leakage of sensitive information.

Reputation and Trust

A cyberattack can severely damage an organization's or an individual's reputation. Trust is crucial in any relationship, whether it's between a business and its customers or among friends and family online. Cybersecurity helps maintain that trust by ensuring data integrity and privacy.

Compliance and Legal Requirements

Numerous regulations and laws mandate the protection of data. Compliance with these requirements by ensuring cybersecurity is not just a legal obligation but also a way to avoid hefty fines and penalties.

National Security

On a larger scale, cybersecurity is crucial for protecting critical infrastructure and maintaining national security. Cyberattacks on government systems or essential services like power grids, water supplies, and electoral results can have devastating consequences.

Cyber Security Demystified: It's Easier Than You Think

We were all made to believe cybersecurity is this complex, mysterious tech stuff reserved for tech wizards. But it's not as complex as we were made to believe. Think of it like everyday safety precautions you already practice without consciously knowing.

Let's look at it this way: setting up strong passwords and changing them regularly is like locking your front door—a basic step that keeps your digital space secure. It doesn't require you to be a techie; it just needs a bit of common sense and consistency.

Those notifications for software updates that frequently appear on your devices—what about them? They're not just for adding new features or fixing bugs. They often include crucial security patches that plug holes hackers could exploit. So, clicking that "update" button is like maintaining your car to prevent breakdowns—it's preventive maintenance in the digital world.

And then there's the golden rule: "think before you click." Just as you wouldn't blindly trust a stranger offering something too good to be true, be cautious online. It's just like being street smart—common sense can go a long way in preventing you from falling victim.

Cybersecurity isn't about mastering complex algorithms or understanding every intricacy of digital threats. It's about adopting sensible habits and staying vigilant. These simple practices form the backbone of cybersecurity. They don't require you to be a tech expert; they need a bit of awareness and proactive effort.

Common Cybersecurity Threats You Need to Know

The digital world is changing along with the online dangers that threaten it. There are several cybersecurity threats, but here are the common ones you need to know:

- **Virus:** This relatively small file can duplicate into another program or file on your computer. A virus can only be transmitted if the host file is shared. Some sophisticated viruses can change themselves to make their detection or removal hard. Viruses usually don't pose a big threat, but few can be very destructive. Luckily, viruses are less common now than before.

- **Malware:** Also called malicious software, malware is a program created to compromise the confidentiality or integrity of a computer or server. It has become one of the most common computer threats and can cause widespread disruption or steal information. Spyware is a common type of malware that has increasingly become a major threat to organizations—it violates privacy, carries out financial fraud, and tracks personal information.

- **Ransomware**: This form of malware prevents you from accessing your files or system. You'll be asked to pay a certain amount using online payment methods to access your system. It encrypts files using public key encryption, with the decryption key only available to the cybercriminal.

- **Phishing:** This cyberattack utilizes social engineering, emails, or social media to lure you into sharing personal information such as account details or passwords. Cybercriminals will pretend to be officials from an organization and share a fake website link where you'll be required to provide sensitive information that will go to the criminal's server.

Mythbusters: Dispelling Common Misconceptions

One of the best ways to ensure you are safe online is to know about common cybersecurity misconceptions and how to avoid them. Here are some common cybersecurity myths:

- **I'm not a target:** Many believe that only large organizations or high-profile individuals are targeted by cybercriminals. In reality, everyone is a potential target. Cybercriminals often go after small businesses and individuals because they usually have weaker security measures.

- **Strong passwords are enough:** Strong passwords are really important, but we need more than just that. Multi-factor authentication (MFA), regular updates, and keeping an eye on things are key parts of a strong security plan. Passwords can be taken, but MFA gives an extra layer of security.

- **Antivirus software will keep me safe:** Antivirus software is a crucial element of cybersecurity but not a silver bullet. It's part of a broader strategy that should include firewalls, regular software updates, and user education on recognizing threats like phishing attempts.

- **I'm wise enough to spot a phishing attempt:** Phishing attacks are becoming more sophisticated every day, making it harder to catch sight of them. Cybercriminals use various tactics to make their attempts look legitimate. Continuous education and awareness are vital to identifying and avoiding these threats.

The Human Firewall: Your Actions Are the First Line of Defense

When it comes to cybersecurity, you are the first line of defense. Think of yourself as a human firewall, actively protecting your digital space. The best way is to create a "security mindset" by developing habits and behaviors that enhance online safety. Here's how you can start building this mindset:

- **Be up to date:** Stay updated about the latest information about cyber threats and the best ways to stay safe online. Follow trusted cybersecurity news sources and stay updated on new threats and vulnerabilities.

- **Be skeptical:** Question everything. Anytime you get any unexpected email or message, even from a known contact, verify its authenticity before clicking on any links or downloading any files.

- **Use complex passwords and multi-factor authentication:** Create unique, strong passwords for each account. Avoid information like birthdays or common things about you that can easily be guessed. Multi-factor authentication (MFA) is like an additional layer of security that requires two or more verification methods.

- **Be mindful of public Wi-Fi:** Be cautious when using public Wi-Fi networks to avoid sharing sensitive information, as they are frequently less secure. If you must use public Wi-Fi, ensure you use a virtual private network (VPN) to secure your internet connection.

- **Think before you click:** One of the simplest yet most effective actions you can take is to think twice before clicking on links, especially in emails, messages, or pop-up ads. Cybercriminals often use enticing links to lure you into downloading malware or revealing personal information.

Cybersecurity now goes beyond the realm of tech experts. It's for everyone who uses the internet, including you. By understanding cybersecurity and why it matters, you're already on your way to building a safer digital life. Remember, the key to cybersecurity lies in simple, consistent habits. By staying informed, using strong passwords, being skeptical of suspicious communications, and thinking before you click, you become a human firewall—your best defense against cyber threats. These basic actions can make a big difference, empowering you to confidently navigate the online world.

In the next chapter, we'll discuss extensively how to build your digital defenses, identify sketchy websites, and secure your device.

Chapter 2:

Building Your Digital Defenses

We have set a foundation for the basics, and now it's time to dive into the nuts and bolts of building your digital defenses. Think of this as setting up a strong fence around your online life. We'll start by taking your password game to another level, ensuring you have strong, complex, yet memorable passwords. We'll also discuss how to utilize two-factor authentication for an extra layer of security. Then, we'll discuss how to surf safely online, teaching you how to spot sketchy websites, dodge phishing scams, and be a savvy social media user.

Next, we'll move on to securing your devices—your computer, smartphone, tablet, and even those smart home gadgets. This chapter will cover these and many more.

Password Power-Up

The cornerstone of cybersecurity is a strong password. Your password is like the front door to your online life; it must be strong enough to keep intruders out. Ensure the security of your online accounts by creating robust passwords. Opt for passwords with 12 to 16 characters that include a mix of uppercase and lowercase letters, numbers, and special characters. For instance, instead of using a simple word like "School," you could create a complex one like "S¢h00l1234!". Avoid anything that can be easily guessed like a name or birth year.

To make your passwords even more secure, consider using phrases. These are just some random words that you can easily remember. This method makes it easier to remember while still being difficult for hackers to crack. Also, try incorporating randomness into your passwords by substituting letters with numbers or symbols, like turning "School" into "S¢h00l1234!". Each account should have its own unique password to ensure that a breach in one account doesn't compromise the others.

Tips for Remembering Complex Passwords

- **Use mnemonics**: Make a simple phrase using the first letters of words combined with numbers and special characters for an easy memory aid. For example, "I love to eat pizza every Friday night at 6" becomes "Il2epFna6!".

- **Chunking:** Break your password into smaller, more digestible parts. For instance, "Xy7!aR3$Tk9!" can be remembered as "Xy7! aR3$ Tk9!". This makes it easier to remember.

- **Repetition:** Regularly typing out your passwords rather than relying solely on autofill can reinforce your recall, helping embed them in your memory over time.

- **Utilize personal associations**: Tie parts of your password to personal memories or associations. For example, use the initials of a favorite song or book, and essential dates or symbols.

What Are Two Factor Authentication (2FA) and How it Works

Two-factor authentication (2FA) serves as an extra lock to your digital front door, providing additional security to your online accounts. Essentially, 2FA requires two forms of identification before granting access. The first is something you know, such as your password, while the second is typically something you have, such as a fingerprint or a face scan.

To proceed, enter your password, then you'll receive a prompt to complete the secondary verification step. This could be a code sent to your mobile phone via text message, an authentication app, or a biometric scan like your fingerprint or face. For example, after typing your password, you might receive a six-digit code on your phone that you need to enter to complete the login process. This means that even if by chance someone guesses your password, they would still need the second factor to access your account.

By using two different forms of identification, 2FA greatly boosts your account's security. It makes it much harder for cybercriminals to break in, as they would need both your password and your second factor, which is typically something only you have access to. This added step might seem like a minor inconvenience, but it greatly reduces the risk of unauthorized access and helps keep your digital life secure.

Understanding the Functionality of Password Managers

We've all had those moments when we can't remember if our password is our pet's name followed by our birth year or something equally obscure. That's where password managers come in handy. They're like your personal vault for all those complex passwords you need to remember but shouldn't write down on sticky notes.

Password managers keep all your passwords safely in one place. Think of it as a digital safe that only you can access with a master password. You just need to remember one strong password instead of many. Plus, they can generate strong, random passwords for you—those impossible-to-crack combinations that even the smartest cybercriminal can't easily guess.

A core advantage of password managers is they work across all your devices, so you're never stranded without your login details. So, if you're tired of the password-guessing game and want to boost your online security without the hassle, a password manager is your new favorite tool.

Safe Surfing 101: How to Identify Sketchy Websites and Avoid Phishing Scams

The internet is so vast that surfing it can feel like exploring uncharted territory. One of the best ways to stay safe is by identifying sketchy websites and being smart enough to escape phishing scams.

How to Identify Sketchy Websites

One of the most crucial things in maintaining your cybersecurity is avoiding fake websites. Sometimes, cybercriminals create websites that look too good to be sketchy; thus, there is a need to always be on the lookout. Here are some tips to help you spot suspicious sites online:

- **Look at the URL carefully:** Always check the website's URL for misspellings or unnecessary characters. For example, "amaz0n.com" instead of "amazon.com" can signify a fake website. Look for "https" at the start of the link, which indicates that the website encrypts your data. While having "https" doesn't ensure total safety, it's a good initial step.

- **Check their contact information:** Reputable websites always provide ways to contact them, like their office address, mobile number, or email. If this information is missing or seems fake, it's a red flag.

- **Check the design and content quality:** Reliable websites typically have professional design and well-written content. Additionally, if the site is overloaded with ads, especially pop-ups, it's likely to be sketchy.

- **Check out the reviews of previous users:** Search for reviews or feedback about the website. Legitimate sites mostly have positive reviews from previous users. If you can't find any information or if you find negative reviews, it's best to avoid the site.

- **Verify security certificates:** Many browsers allow you to view a website's security certificate. Click on the padlock symbol in the browser's address bar to see who issued the certificate. Legitimate sites will have certificates issued by recognized authorities.

Tips to Avoid Phishing Scams

Cybercriminals try to trick you into giving them your private information, such as passwords, credit card numbers, and personal data. Here are some strategies to keep you safe:

- **Be skeptical of unexpected emails or messages:** Always question unexpected emails, especially those that ask for private information, prompt you to click a link, or urge you to take immediate action. Phishers often create a sense of urgency to get you to act without thinking.

- **Check the sender's email address carefully:** Examine the sender's email address closely. Scammers often use addresses similar to legitimate ones but may have slight variations, like extra numbers or misspelled domains.

- **Be cautious of non-personalized greetings:** Phishing scammers typically begin their messages with generic salutations such as "Dear Customer" instead of addressing individuals by their actual names. Legitimate companies usually personalize their communication.

- **Avoid clicking on every link sent to you:** Check links in emails to see where they lead. Don't click if the URL looks suspicious or doesn't match the legitimate site's address.

- **Always verify with the source:** If you receive a dubious email that appears to be from a company you do business with, contact the company directly using a known and trusted method. Avoid using the contact information shared in the email.

Device Lockdown: Securing Your Computer, Smartphone, Tablet, and Smart Home Devices

One of the most essential cybersecurity measures is to secure your devices. Whether it's your computer, smartphone, tablet, or smart home device, each plays a crucial role in your digital life and deserves adequate protection. Let's look at some practical steps to keep each of them secure.

Computer

Be sure to regularly update your computer's operating system and software. These updates often have important security fixes that keep your computer safe from new online threats. Install a reputable antivirus program and keep it updated, too. Also, set up your firewall to block illegal access to your devices.

Smartphones and Tablets

These devices are mini-computers that we carry everywhere, and they store a lot of our personal information. Use a complex, unique password to lock your screen. Better yet, enable biometric security, like fingerprint or facial recognition, if your device supports it. Exercise caution when selecting and installing applications on your device. Remember to regularly update the operating system and applications on your device, just as you would with a computer.

Smart Home Devices

Smart home devices makes things a lot easier for us; but they also come with security risks. Change default passwords on these devices to something strong and unique. Set up a separate network for your smart devices to isolate them from your primary devices, like computers and phones. This way, even if a hacker gets into your smart phone, they won't automatically have access to your laptop.

Be careful with your home Wi-Fi. Use a strong, unique password for your network and enable WPA3 encryption if your router supports it. Only devices that are trusted can connect to your network.

Data Defender: Safeguarding Your Precious Information

Your digital information is like precious jewels—you wouldn't just leave it lying around unprotected, would you? Just like valuable possessions, your data needs protection, too, so you've got to be your own "Data Defender." Let's look at some essential data-defending tips to help you safeguard your digital information:

Backups

Backups work like your data's safety net. In case of a cyber threat, system failure, or accidental deletion, having a backup means you won't lose your important files. Ensure you regularly backup your data to a cloud storage or external hard drive. This way, even if something happens to your primary device, you'll have a copy of everything you need safely stored elsewhere.

Encryption

Encryption is like putting your data in a secure vault. When data is encrypted, it gets converted into a code that can only be accessed by someone with the correct key or password. This means that even if a hacker intercepts your data, they won't be able to read it without the decryption key. Enable encryption on your devices and use encrypted communication methods, especially for sensitive information like financial transactions and personal details.

Privacy Settings

Privacy settings are your way of controlling who can access your information. Social media platforms, apps, and even your operating systems offer privacy settings that let you decide what you share and with whom. Review and adjust these settings. Limit the personal information you share publicly, and be careful about app permissions. It's all about having control over your digital information and ensuring you're the only one who can access your data.

We've discussed a lot about building your digital defenses, and by now, it's clear that a few key strategies can significantly bolster your online security. We've emphasized the importance of setting strong, memorable passwords and using two-factor authentication for extra protection. We've also highlighted the role of password managers in simplifying and securing your online credentials.

In addition to securing your accounts, we've covered how to safely navigate the internet by identifying sketchy websites and avoiding phishing scams. Remember to be your data defender by regularly backing up your data, encrypting sensitive information, and adjusting your privacy settings. By implementing these measures, you're on your way to securing your digital space and ready to withstand potential cyber threats.

Chapter 3:

Cybersecurity on the Go

In today's world, being constantly connected is almost necessary—whether working from a cozy café, catching up on emails while waiting for a flight, or simply browsing on the go. But with this convenience comes a host of cybersecurity risks. This chapter will discuss keeping your digital life secure while you're out. We'll explore the hidden dangers of public Wi-Fi, provide tips for safeguarding your devices and data while traveling, and guide you on what to do if your device gets lost or stolen.

Imagine sitting in a bustling airport or a trendy coffee shop, unaware that your free Wi-Fi could be a hacker's playground. Or consider the chaos of losing your phone or laptop while on a business trip. These scenarios highlight the importance of being proactive about mobile cybersecurity. By the end of this chapter, you'll be equipped with practical knowledge to keep your digital defenses strong, no matter where you are. So, buckle up and get ready to strengthen your mobile security against the threats of the digital world.

Wi-Fi Woes: Public Wi-Fi Risks and How to Use it Safely

Public Wi-Fi can be a lifesaver when you're out and about, offering free internet access at cafes, airports, hotels, and other public places. Public Wi-Fi networks are risky as they are often not secure, making them easy targets for hackers who can steal your information. When you connect to a public Wi-Fi network, you share a space with hundreds of other users. Malicious criminals can eavesdrop on your online activities without proper security measures, steal personal information, or even inject malware into your device. That's why it's crucial to be cautious and take steps to protect yourself whenever you're using these networks. In this section, we'll discuss the risks associated with public Wi-Fi and provide tips on using it safely to enjoy the convenience without compromising your security.

Risks of Using Public Wi-Fi

No one has told you this before, but connecting to a public Wi-Fi is like broadcasting your personal information to anyone within range. Here are some common risks of using public Wi-Fi:

- **Data interception:** When you use public Wi-Fi, your data is transmitted through the airwaves. Hackers can intercept this data using special software, gaining access to sensitive information like passwords, credit card numbers, and personal messages. It's similar to someone eavesdropping on your conversation at a crowded café.

- **Man-in-the-middle attacks:** This is a sneaky method in which a hacker positions themselves between you and the network you're trying to connect to. This allows them to monitor your online activities, steal personal data, or even alter the communication between you and the websites you visit without your knowledge. It's like having an unwanted third party listen in and alter your conversations without you realizing it.

- **Fake Wi-Fi networks:** Cybercriminals can create fake Wi-Fi networks that look like real ones to fool people into connecting. Once connected, they can easily access your device and steal sensitive information.

- **Malware distribution:** Unsecured public Wi-Fi networks can be used to spread malware. Hackers can insert malicious software into your device, which can then steal your information, track your activities, or even take control of your device. Think of this as picking up a beautifully wrapped gift on the street only to find it filled with harmful content.

How to Use Public Wi-Fi Safely

Here are some tips to help you stay safe while connecting to public Wi-Fi networks:

- **Consider using a VPN:** A Virtual Private Network (VPN) encrypts your internet connection, making it much harder for anyone on the same network to access your data.

- **Avoid sensitive transactions:** Avoid online banking, shopping, or entering sensitive information while connected to public Wi-Fi. If you must, ensure the website is secured.

- **Forget the network after use:** After using the public Wi-Fi, disconnect and tell your device to forget the network. This prevents automatic reconnection in the future and reduces the risk of your device being exposed.

- **Turn off sharing:** When using public Wi-Fi, turn off file sharing, printer sharing, and other sharing settings on your device. This minimizes the chances of others accessing your files or data.

- **Use security software:** Install and run reliable security software on your device. It easily detects and blocks potential threats from unsecured networks.

Travel Tips: Protecting Your Devices and Data While on the Road

Ensuring your device's safety is not just important at home; it becomes even more critical when you're out experiencing the excitement of the world. Traveling comes with some unique challenges for keeping your devices and data safe. Whether exploring a new city or attending a work conference, ensuring digital security is crucial. In this section, we'll walk you through some practical tips to protect your gadgets and personal information so you can focus on enjoying your trip without the added worry of cyber threats.

- **Ensure all your devices are secured**: Use strong passwords or biometric locks (like fingerprint or facial recognition) on your devices. This serves as a layer of security in case your phone or laptop gets lost or stolen.

- **Always keep your devices with you:** Always keep your devices within sight, especially in crowded places or on public transport. If you must leave them unattended, use a secure, lockable bag or compartment.

- **Use secure connections:** Avoid connecting to unknown or unsecured Wi-Fi networks. If you need to go online, use your phone's data connection or a trusted VPN to ensure your connection is encrypted.

- **Back up all your data meticulously:** Before you travel, back up important data to the cloud or an external hard drive. This way, you won't lose valuable information if your device is damaged.

- **Steer clear of public charging stations:** Avoid public charging stations to prevent potential malware on your device. Instead, use your charger and plug it into a power outlet.

- **Enable Find My Device:** Activate location tracking features on your devices (like Find My iPhone or Find My Device on Android) so you can locate them if they go missing.

- **Be wary of public Wi-Fi:** We've explained this above, but it can't be overemphasized that public networks can be risky. If you want to protect important information, use a VPN to keep your data safe from people who try to see it without permission.

Lost or Stolen Device: What to Do and How to Minimize the Damage

Losing a device or having it stolen can be stressful, but knowing the proper steps can help you minimize the damage and protect your information. Let's take you through the right actions you should take if you lose your device, from securing your accounts to tracking your device. Here are some tips to follow to reduce the risk of unauthorized access and potentially recover your device:

- **Track your device:** This has to top our list. Keep going even when you lose your device; use tracking apps like Find My iPhone or Find My Device to locate your device. This can help you determine if it's nearby or if it's been moved.

- **Remotely lock the device:** Access your tracking app to lock the device remotely, enhancing data security to block unauthorized access and discourage potential intruders.

- **Send a message:** Send a message to your device with your contact information. If someone finds it, they might return it to you.

- **Erase your data:** If recovery seems unlikely or you feel your device is in the wrong hands, use the tracking app to erase all data. Safeguard your personal data to prevent unauthorized access or misuse.

- **Change your passwords:** To prevent unauthorized access, update the passwords for all accounts accessible from the lost device, including email, banking, and social media accounts.

- **Notify your service provider:** Inform your service provider about the loss. They can suspend or deactivate your account, which helps prevent your device from being used for fraud.

- **Report the loss to authorities:** File a report with local authorities, providing details like serial numbers and tracking information. This can help recover the device and address potential misuse.

- **Monitor your accounts**: Keep a close look on your financial and personal accounts for any unusual activity. Report any suspicious transactions or logins immediately to the relevant institutions.

Keeping your online accounts safe when using your devices away from home is very important. By being aware of the risks associated with public Wi-Fi, following best practices for protecting your devices while traveling, and knowing the steps to take if your device is lost or stolen, you can significantly reduce your exposure to cybersecurity threats. These precautions safeguard your personal information and enhance your overall peace of mind as you navigate various online and offline environments.

Ultimately, staying vigilant and proactive about cybersecurity while on the go ensures that you can enjoy the convenience of staying connected without compromising your safety. By implementing the strategies we have discussed in this chapter, you're fully equipped to handle potential risks. You can focus on what truly matters—exploring new places, catching up with friends, or simply staying productive while away from home.

Chapter 4:

When Things Go Wrong

You might take all the necessary steps to fortify your digital space, but something can still slip through the cracks. This chapter will guide you through what to do when the unexpected happens, serving as your emergency handbook for digital mishaps.

First, we'll help you identify the red flags that indicate your security has been compromised. Next, we'll cover immediate steps to take if you suspect a breach, helping you to act swiftly and minimize damage. Then, we'll discuss how to fight back by reporting cybercrime and utilizing available resources. Lastly, we'll help you assemble your cybersecurity toolkit—a simple, effective plan to strengthen defenses and respond to threats confidently.

Signs of Trouble: How to Know if You've Been Hacked or if Your Device Is Compromised

It's a beautiful evening; you're working on your computer or scrolling through your phone, and everything seems normal. But then, things start to feel off. Maybe your phone or laptop is acting weird, or you notice fishy activities on your accounts. Could it be that you've been hacked? Recognizing the signs of a compromised device or account is essential for taking quick action and preventing further damage. Here are some red flags that might indicate your device is hacked:

- **Unexpected pop-ups:** If you're suddenly seeing a lot of pop-up ads or strange notifications, it might be a sign that your device is infected with malware. In most cases, these pop-ups lead you to malicious sites that can add malware to your device.

- **Slow performance:** A device hacked or infected with malware often runs slower than usual. This can be due to malicious programs running in the background, using your device's resources.

- **Unusual activity:** Be on the lookout for unusual activities on your accounts. This could be emails sent from your account that you didn't write, posts on your social media that you didn't make, or purchases on your credit card that you didn't authorize.

- **Password issues:** If you're suddenly locked out of your accounts or receiving password reset emails you didn't request, it's a strong indicator that someone might have gained access to your device.

- **New programs or files**: Always look for new programs or files on your device that you didn't install. Hackers often install software to help them maintain access or spy on your activities.

- **Strange browser behavior:** If your browser's homepage has changed, new toolbars appear, or you're being redirected to different websites, it might be compromised.

Damage Control: Immediate Steps to Take if You Suspect a Breach

It can really be scary to notice some suspicious activities on your device or accounts indicating you might have been hacked. Don't panic! The key is to act quickly and efficiently to minimize the damage. Here are the immediate steps you should take if you suspect a breach on your devices:

- **Go offline:** The first thing you should do is disconnect from the internet. This prevents further data from being sent or received by malicious software on your device. If you're on Wi-Fi, turn it off or disconnect the cable if you're wired.

- **Change your passwords:** Immediately change the passwords for your critical accounts, such as email, banking, and social media. If you think your primary device is compromised, use a different device. Ensure the new passwords are unique and secure.

- **Enable two-factor authentication (2FA):** Requesting a second verification form beyond your password is an additional security layer.

- **Scan for malware:** Use an antivirus program to scan your device for malware. If any threats are detected, follow the software's instructions to quarantine or remove them. This step can help identify and eliminate the malicious software causing the breach.

- **Update your software:** Ensure your operating system and all applications are up-to-date. Software updates come with security patches that cover up the vulnerabilities hackers might take advantage of.

- **Review account activity:** Review recent activity on your important accounts. Check for any unfamiliar logins, changes to passwords, or transactions that seem suspicious. Report any suspicious activity to the respective service providers immediately.

- **Notify the right parties:** If sensitive information, such as your email or financial details, may have been exposed, inform your email provider, bank, or credit card company. They can help monitor for fraud and provide additional security measures.

- **Backup important data:** If your device is still operational, back up your important files to an external hard drive or cloud storage. This ensures you don't lose your data if you need to reset or replace your device.

- **Consult a professional:** If you're unsure about your next steps or the breach seems severe, consult a cybersecurity professional. They can provide expert advice and assistance to secure your systems.

- **Report the incident:** Depending on the severity, you might need to report the breach to local authorities or a cybercrime unit. They can conduct a thorough investigation to prevent similar incidents from occurring in the future.

- **Monitor your accounts:** For the next few weeks, monitor your accounts closely. Look for any signs of unauthorized access or transactions and promptly report any new suspicious activity.

Fighting Back: Reporting Cybercrime and Resources for Victims

You've just realized that you're a victim of cybercrime. It's frustrating, maybe even a little frightening, but you're not alone, and there are steps you can take to fight back.

Reporting cybercrime and knowing where to turn for help can make a huge difference in handling the aftermath and preventing further issues. Here's how you can effectively report cybercrime and what resources are available to support you.

- **Recognize the crime:** Firstly, it's important to identify and understand the type of cybercrime you've experienced. Whether it is identity theft, hacking, phishing, or online fraud, knowing the nature of the crime will help you report it accurately and seek the right help.

- **Gather evidence:** Before filing a report, gather all relevant evidence. This could include screenshots of suspicious emails or messages, transaction records, and logs of any unusual activity on your accounts. The more information you have, the easier it is for authorities to investigate.

- **Report law enforcement agents:** Contact your local police department. Many police departments have specialized cybercrime units or officers trained to handle such cases. Provide them with all the evidence and details about the incident. This step is crucial as it creates an official crime record, which can be important for further investigations or insurance claims.

- **Notify the affected parties:** Contact your bank or credit card company immediately if the cybercrime involves your financial information. They can help secure your accounts, monitor for fraudulent transactions, and may issue new cards if necessary. Similarly, if your email or social media accounts are compromised, inform the service providers so they can help restore and secure your accounts.

- **Report to national cybercrime agencies:** In addition to local authorities, you should report the crime to national cybercrime agencies. The Internet Crime Complaint Center (IC3) in the United States helps report online crimes. In the UK, Action Fraud deals with these reports. These agencies specialize in cybercrimes and can coordinate with international authorities if needed.

- **Utilize online platforms:** Several online platforms offer tools for reporting cybercrimes. Websites like Cybercrime Support Network (cybercrimesupport.org) provide resources and guidance for reporting online crimes. They also offer support for victims and ease the recovery process.

- **Seek the help of a lawyer:** Consider seeking a lawyer with expertise in cyber law. They can provide legal advice on protecting your rights, recovering damages, and taking any necessary legal action against the perpetrators.

- **Stay informed:** Educate yourself about cyber threats and ways to protect against them. Many cybersecurity organizations offer free resources, webinars, and newsletters to update you on the latest threats and prevention strategies.

Resources for Victims

Here are some resources that can help if you fall victim to cybercrime:

- **Identity Theft Resource Center (idtheftcenter.org):** This organization helps people who have had their identity stolen. They give advice on what to do to get better and how to stop it from happening again.

- **Cybercrime Support Network (cybercrimesupport.org):** This organization offers resources and support for various cybercrimes and helps victims understand their options.

- **Federal Trade Commission (ftc.gov):** For Americans, it offers a comprehensive guide on dealing with identity theft and other cybercrimes.

- **National Cyber Security Centre (ncsc.gov.uk):** This center supports those dealing with cyber incidents in the UK.

Your Cybersecurity Toolkit: Simple Steps to Create Your Security Plan

A whole cybersecurity plan? That sounds daunting, but with the right guidance, it's quite straightforward. It's simply putting together a toolkit that helps you stay safe in the digital world. We've discussed most of the points throughout our journey in this book, but let's bring everything together to make it a personal cybersecurity toolkit:

Assess Your Current Security

First, we've got to look at where you are right now. Review your current security measures: Are your passwords strong? Do you use two-factor authentication? Have you updated your software recently? This self-assessment will give you a clear idea of where to improve.

Strong Passwords and a Password Manager

As we've said before, passwords are your first line of defense. Ensure all your passwords are complex and unique. An excellent way to manage all your passwords in one place is by using a password manager. This tool stores all your passwords securely and can generate complex ones for you, so you don't have to remember each one.

Enable Two-Factor Authentication (2FA)

Two-factor authentication adds a layer of security. It requires you to provide a second verification form, like a code sent to your phone, in addition to your password. Having 2FA on your accounts makes it harder for anyone to gain illegal access.

Regular Software Updates

It's really important to regularly update your software. Updates often include fixes for security issues that hackers could use. If possible, set your devices to update automatically so you don't miss any important fixes.

Backup Your Data

Regular backups are essential to protect against data loss from malware, hardware failure, or other disasters. Use both physical backups (like an external hard drive) and cloud backups to ensure you always have access to your important files.

Use Encryption

Encryption is like locking up all your data in a secret vault that only you can access. It scrambles your information so that even if someone intercepts it, they can't read it without the encryption key. Ensure you enable encryption on your devices and use encrypted communication methods, especially for sensitive data.

Privacy Settings

Adjust the settings on your social media and devices to control what you share and who can see it. Be careful about app permissions and restrict access to your personal info.

Secure Your Wi-Fi

Your home Wi-Fi is the gateway to your entire network. Use a complex password for your Wi-Fi network and set up WPA3 encryption if your router supports it. This helps keep unwanted visitors out. Also, be wary of using public Wi-Fi.

Utilize Antivirus and Anti-Malware Software

Install antivirus software on your devices. These programs can detect and remove malicious software, protecting your system from a wide range of threats. Keep them updated to ensure they can defend against the latest viruses and malware.

Be on the Lookout for Phishing Scams

Always be cautious with emails, messages, and links. Check who's sending the message and don't open any strange links or files from people you don't know.

Educate Yourself

Cybersecurity is an ongoing process. Stay updated about the latest threats and the best ways to avoid them. Regularly check cybersecurity blogs, subscribe to newsletters, or read books on cybersecurity.

Have a Recovery Plan

Even with the best precautions, breaches can still happen. Have a plan for what to do if your data gets hacked. This includes knowing how to report the breach, who to contact, and the steps to secure your accounts.

Having a plan when things go wrong can make all the difference. This chapter discussed recognizing signs of trouble, taking immediate action to mitigate damage, and reporting cybercrime. We've also highlighted key resources to support you during a cyber crisis.

Creating your cybersecurity toolkit keeps you proactive and prepared. Regularly assessing your security, using strong passwords, enabling two-factor authentication, and keeping your software up-to-date can significantly reduce the risk of cyber threats. Remember, the digital world constantly evolves, and staying educated and vigilant can never be overemphasized. The next chapter will provide you with reputable sources to stay informed about cybercrime threats and online communities where you can learn and connect.

Chapter 5:

Stay Ahead of the Game

Just like in a game, keeping up with the latest moves and strategies is key to staying secure. This chapter will focus on staying ahead in the ever-evolving landscape of cybersecurity. We will guide you on how to stay informed about new threats, connect with cybersecurity communities, and commit to lifelong learning.

First, we'll explore reputable sources for the latest cybersecurity news. Next, we'll discuss the importance of cybersecurity buddies—online communities and forums where you can learn from like-minded individuals, share your experiences, and build a supportive network. Read on to discover how you can stay ahead of the game and maintain a strong defense in the digital world.

News You Can Use: Reputable Sources for Staying Informed About Threats

Keeping up-to-date with the latest cybersecurity threats is extremely important. The world of cyber threats is constantly changing, with new vulnerabilities and attack methods emerging regularly. You must know what's happening in real time to keep your defenses strong. Here are sites to follow for up-to-date and reliable information on cybersecurity threats:

Krebs on Security

Founded by journalist Brian Krebs, this site is renowned for its in-depth investigative reporting on cybersecurity breaches, malware, and cybercriminal activities. It offers detailed articles, news updates, and insights into cybersecurity threats and trends.

Dark Reading

This site is a comprehensive resource for IT security professionals. Dark Reading provides its visitors with well-researched articles, fact checked analyses, and latest news on cybersecurity topics. You can find industry news, threat intelligence, and expert opinions on emerging security threats and defenses.

Bleeping Computer

Founded over 20 years ago, this community-driven site offers news, technical support, and information on various cybersecurity issues, from ransomware to software vulnerabilities. Bleeping Computer includes tutorials, security news, and forums for discussing cybersecurity problems and solutions.

The Hacker News

As one of the leading cybersecurity news platforms, The Hacker News covers the latest hacking news, cyber-attacks, vulnerabilities, and data breaches. The site updates cybersecurity incidents, technology news, and expert analysis daily.

SANS Internet Storm Center

Operated by the SANS Institute, this site provides real-time analysis and alerts on emerging cybersecurity threats. It features incident reports, threat analysis, and educational resources for security professionals.

CSO Online

Aimed at chief security officers and security decision-makers, CSO Online offers news, analysis, and research on information security. It has articles about managing cybersecurity, keeping data safe, and identifying threats.

MITRE CVE

This is the official source for Common Vulnerabilities and Exposures (CVE) data, providing a standardized list of publicly known cybersecurity vulnerabilities. It includes detailed information on CVEs, such as descriptions, references, and tips on avoiding becoming a victim.

NIST National Vulnerability Database (NVD)

The National Institute of Standards and Technology manages the NVD, including CVE entries, additional analysis, references, and metrics. It offers comprehensive vulnerability data, including impact scores and severity ratings.

CVE Details

This renowned site aggregates CVE data and provides detailed statistics and analysis on vulnerabilities. CVE Details is a searchable database of CVEs, trends, and statistics on vulnerabilities across different platforms and products.

SecurityFocus (Symantec)

One of the early sources for cybersecurity news and vulnerability information, SecurityFocus has been less active in recent years but still offers valuable resources. It includes vulnerability databases, security advisories, and expert analysis on cybersecurity threats.

Cybersecurity Buddies: Online Communities and Forums Where You Can Learn and Connect

A good way to enhance your cybersecurity knowledge is by exploring online communities and forums to connect with others in the field. Here are some online communities to connect and learn more about cybersecurity:

Reddit - r/cybersecurity

This subreddit is a vibrant forum where cybersecurity enthusiasts and professionals gather to discuss a wide range of topics related to security. Discussions cover everything from the latest vulnerabilities and security trends to career advice and educational resources. You'll find threads on recent breaches, new security tools, and best practices for various aspects of cybersecurity. The active user base ensures constantly updated information and diverse opinions. You are encouraged to inquire, impart your knowledge, and engage in discussions on current topics. It's an excellent place for learning and staying informed about cybersecurity.

Stack Exchange - Information Security

Stack Exchange's Information Security site is a specialized Q&A platform focusing on the technical aspects of cybersecurity. It provides detailed answers to complex security questions, discussions about security protocols, and explanations of security vulnerabilities and mitigation strategies. The quality of answers is typically high due to community moderation and the focus on precise, technical content. It's particularly useful if you have specific technical questions or need in-depth explanations of security concepts.

Spiceworks - Security Forum

Spiceworks is a community for IT professionals with a dedicated section for security discussions. Here, you can engage in conversations about security tools, incident management, and network protection. Users often share their experiences with different security products and offer practical advice on handling security incidents. The forum also includes reviews and recommendations for security products. The blend of professional insights and product reviews makes it a valuable resource for learning about security practices and finding recommendations for security solutions. It's a good resource for understanding real-world applications of security tools.

Cybersecurity Insiders

Cybersecurity Insiders is a platform for cybersecurity professionals. It offers industry news, career advice, and discussions on emerging threats and technologies. The site features insights from experts and updates on the latest trends in cybersecurity. It's geared towards professionals looking to advance their careers and staying updated on industry developments. The platform offers news, professional advice, and discussions on cutting-edge security issues, making it a comprehensive resource for professionals.

Discord - Cybersecurity Servers

Discord hosts multiple servers dedicated to cybersecurity, providing a platform for real-time discussions. These servers offer channels for chatting about different security topics, sharing resources, and collaborating on projects. You can engage in live discussions, seek immediate feedback, and join groups working on security-related projects. The real-time chat format allows for spontaneous discussions and quick exchanges of information. It's an informal and interactive way to engage with others and get immediate responses to your queries.

Lifelong Learning: The Importance of Staying Up-To-Date on Cybersecurity Trends

Keeping up with cybersecurity trends isn't just for IT professionals—it's crucial for everyone who wants to protect their online presence. Here's why staying informed about the latest cybersecurity developments is important for you:

Preventing Common Threats

Cyber threats like phishing scams, malware, and ransomware are common and constantly evolving. By staying updated on these trends, you can learn to recognize suspicious emails, avoid malicious links, and use the latest security tools to protect yourself. For instance, recognizing a phishing email can help you avoid disclosing personal information accidentally.

Using Up-to-Date Security Tools

Security tools and software are updated regularly to be fit enough to address new vulnerabilities and threats. Updating your antivirus, firewall, and web browser regularly helps you stay protected with the latest security features. Learning about new security features and updates helps you make sure your tools are working effectively to keep you safe.

Understanding New Privacy Practices

As online privacy concerns grow, new privacy practices and settings are continually being introduced. Staying informed about these changes helps you manage your privacy settings more effectively, ensuring your personal information remains secure. For instance, having a good understanding of your social media privacy settings can help you control who sees your information.

Recognizing Scams and Fraud

Online scams and fraud schemes are always changing. Being updated about the latest types of scams can protect you from falling victim to them. Awareness of common scams, such as fake tech support calls or fraudulent investment schemes, allows you to spot red flags and avoid potential losses.

Safe Online Behavior

Staying updated on cybersecurity trends also helps you adopt safer online behaviors. For example, learning about the importance of using strong, unique passwords and enabling two-factor authentication can significantly reduce your risk of being hacked. Understanding these practices helps you take proactive steps to secure your online accounts.

Protecting Personal Information

As data breaches and identity theft become more common, knowing how to protect your personal information is crucial. Staying informed about the latest threats and best practices for data security helps you safeguard sensitive information like financial details and personal identification numbers.

Adapting to New Technologies

Technology is constantly advancing, and new devices and applications are introduced every day. Staying updated on cybersecurity trends helps you understand how to secure new technologies, such as smart home devices and mobile apps, which can sometimes pose new security risks.

Being Prepared for Online Risks

Regularly learning about cybersecurity trends keeps you prepared for potential online risks. Whether you need to understand how to handle a data breach or react if your accounts are compromised, staying informed ensures you're ready to take appropriate action and minimize any damage.

It's very important to stay updated in the quickly changing world of cybersecurity. Just as in any game where success depends on understanding the latest strategies, your ability to stay secure online depends on keeping up with new threats and solutions. By checking reputable sources for cybersecurity news and participating in online communities, you can stay informed and effectively protect yourself against evolving cyber risks.

Conclusion

We've come to the end of our journey, so let's take a moment to reflect on all we've discussed. Cybersecurity can seem daunting, filled with jargon and complex concepts, but hopefully, this book has demystified much of that for you. The goal of this guide was to provide you with straightforward, actionable advice that you can easily integrate into your daily life.

We began by learning the basic ideas of cybersecurity—why it's important and how it can affect anyone. We then moved on to Chapter 1, where we broke down cybersecurity basics, explored common threats, and debunked myths, emphasizing the role of individuals as the first line of defense. In Chapter 2, we covered essential strategies for securing your online presence, including strong passwords, safe browsing habits, and device security.

Chapter 3 discussed the unique challenges of staying secure while traveling, using public Wi-Fi, and what to do if your device is lost or stolen. Chapter 4 focused on recognizing signs of a breach, immediate steps to mitigate damage, and how to report and recover from cyber incidents. Rounding up in Chapter 5, we explored ways to stay informed about emerging threats, the value of online cybersecurity communities, and the importance of continuous learning in this ever-evolving field.

Creating a habit of cybersecurity doesn't require a massive overhaul of your daily life. It's about integrating small, consistent actions that, over time, build a strong line of defense. Regularly update your software and devices. It might seem tedious, but these updates are crucial for fixing security vulnerabilities. Also, ensure your passwords are long, unique, and difficult to guess. Use a password manager to keep your passwords safe and easily accessible. Don't forget to add an extra layer of security to your accounts by enabling two-factor authentication, making it harder for hackers to gain access. Be careful before you click on links or download files, especially if you don't know where they're from. A moment of caution can prevent a lot of trouble.

So, what's the first step? Start small. Maybe it's updating your passwords this week, setting up two-factor authentication next week, and gradually building up your defenses. The key is to make these actions a part of your routine, just like locking your front door.

By incorporating these steps into your daily routine, you're building a habit that will protect you in the long run. It's like brushing your teeth—small actions, repeated regularly, that make a big difference.

We understand the world of cybersecurity might seem overwhelming, but remember, you're not alone. You've taken significant steps by educating yourself, and that's something to be proud of. This book has provided you with the tools and knowledge to navigate the digital world safely. The power to protect yourself lies in your hands, and your role is crucial in the fight against cyber threats.

Be proactive and stay updated. Cyber threats are always changing, but so are the ways to fight against them. Engage with online communities, remain updated on the latest news, and don't hesitate to seek help when needed. The more you learn, the stronger your defenses will become.

You've got this! By taking control of your online security, you're safeguarding not just your data but your peace of mind. Cybersecurity is a journey that never ends. Keep moving forward, stay vigilant, and trust in your ability to protect yourself. Your digital life is now a safer place, thanks to your efforts and commitment to cybersecurity.

Appendices

Let's wrap it all with a bonus of some additional resources that can further aid your journey to cybersecurity. Whether you need to decode tech jargon or seek further assistance, this section has you covered.

Cybersecurity Jargon Buster: A Glossary of Terms Explained in Plain English

The cybersecurity lingo can feel like a whole new language. Here's a quick glossary to help you understand some common terms used in this book:

- **Antivirus:** Software designed to detect and remove malicious software.

- **Encryption:** Conversion of data into a code to prevent unauthorized access.

- **Firewall:** A system that blocks unauthorized access to your computer while allowing legitimate communication.

- **Malware:** Harmful software designed to damage or take advantage of any device that can run programs.

- **Phishing:** A fraudulent attempt to obtain sensitive information by disguising it as a trustworthy entity.

- **Ransomware:** Malware that encrypts your data and demands payment for its release.

- **Social engineering:** Manipulating people into giving up confidential information.

- **Spyware:** Software that secretly monitors and collects user activity information.

- **Virtual Private Network (VPN):** A service that encrypts your internet connection, providing privacy and security.

- **Worm**: Worm is a type of harmful software that copies itself and moves from one computer to another.

Need More Help? Resources for Further Information and Support

If you need more in-depth assistance or want to stay updated on the latest in cybersecurity, here are some valuable resources to check out:

- **Cybersecurity and Infrastructure Security Agency (CISA):** Offers comprehensive guides and alerts on cybersecurity threats. (https://www.cisa.gov)

- **National Cyber Security Centre (NCSC):** Provides support for dealing with cyber incidents in the UK (https://www.ncsc.gov.uk)

- **Internet Crime Complaint Center (IC3):** A platform dedicated to reporting online criminal activities within the United States. (https://www.ic3.gov)

- **Krebs on Security:** A cybersecurity expert, Brian Krebs's blog covers the latest threats and tips. (https://krebsonsecurity.com)

- **Cyber Aware:** UK government's campaign offering tips on staying secure online. (https://www.cyberaware.gov.uk)

- **SANS Institute:** Provides cybersecurity training and certifications. (https://www.sans.org)

- **Cybercrime Support Network:** Offers resources and support for various types of cybercrime.(https://www.cybercrimesupport.org)

Remember, cybersecurity is an ongoing process, so this book is just the beginning of your journey. Stay informed, keep your defenses up, and don't hesitate to seek help when needed. Your digital safety is worth the effort!

References

Baker, K. (2024, May 14). *10 most common types of cyber attacks today.* CrowdStrike. https://www.crowdstrike.com/cybersecurity-101/cyberattacks/most-common-types-of-cyberattacks/#3.%20Phishing

Division of Banks. (2024). *Know the types of cyber threats.* Mass.gov. https://www.mass.gov/info-details/know-the-types-of-cyber-threats

Evans, K. (2023, May 23). *The best CVE sources and cyber security news: stay informed and secure.* LinkedIn. https://www.linkedin.com/pulse/best-cve-sources-cyber-security-news-stay-informed-secure-evans-

Shea, S. (2021, August). *What is cybersecurity? Everything you need to know.* TechTarget. https://www.techtarget.com/searchsecurity/definition/cybersecurity

Simplilearn. (2024, May 9). *Introduction to cyber security.* Simplilearn. https://www.simplilearn.com/introduction-to-cyber-security-article#:~:text=Cyber%20Security%20is%20a%20process

Stouffer, C. (2021, June 21). *Is my phone hacked? 5 signs + protection tips.* Norton. https://us.norton.com/blog/malware/is-my-phone-hacked

The importance of staying on top of cybersecurity trends. (2024, January 26). Corporate Vision. https://www.corporatevision-news.com/the-importance-of-staying-on-top-of-cybersecurity-trends/

Toohil, R. (2023, November 17). *How to identify fake websites: 11 warning signs to know.* Aura. https://www.aura.com/learn/how-to-identify-fake-websites

Toohil, R. (2024, February 21). *How to tell if a website is fake: 12 warning signs.* Identity Guard. https://www.identityguard.com/news/how-to-tell-if-a-website-is-fake

Why cybersecurity matters. (n.d.). Maryville University. https://online.maryville.edu/online-masters-degrees/cyber-security/resources/why-cyber-security-matters/

Woollacott, E. (2024, April 14). *6 ways to tell if your phone is hacked - and what to do next.* Forbes. https://www.forbes.com/sites/technology/article/how-to-know-if-your-phone-is-hacked/

www.ingramcontent.com/pod-product-compliance
Lightning Source LLC
LaVergne TN
LVHW081532050326
832903LV00025B/1761